REJOICES

THE WORLD REJOICES

THE GOOD
NEWS OF
CHRISTMAS
DEVOTIONAL

BY

ELIZA HUIE

CYNDI LOGSDON

BROOK TAYLOR

ASHLEY AREY

FOREWORD BY
DAVID PLATT

New Growth Press, Greensboro, NC 27401

"Some of God's Promises for his People" (pp 2-3) was adapted from a list compiled by Dan Flynn, https://godcangodcares.com/54-promises-god-has-made-to-me/.

Cover, Illustrations, Design, and Typesetting: Alecia Sharp

ISBN 978-1-64507-423-6 (Print)
ISBN 978-1-64507-424-3 (eBook)

Library of Congress Cataloging-in-Publication Data on file

Printed in Canada
31 30 29 28 27 26 25 24   1 2 3 4 5

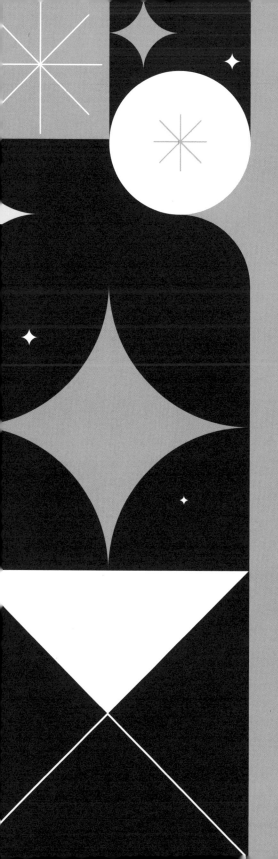

Dedicated to the
McLean Bible Church
family, this book stands
as an acknowledgment
of the profound impact
their love has had
on its authors.

By this everyone will
know that you are my
disciples, if you love one
another. John 13:35

TABLE OF CONTENTS

I am so excited about the book you are holding in your hands. This Christmas devotional is a guided journey through the first two chapters of the gospel of Luke intended to help you and your family know and love Jesus more.

You will find 24 days of thoughtful devotional readings designed to help you slow down and focus your heart and mind on him. The 25th day is a review of the Christmas story in Scripture.

It's my hope that this book will remind you that God was faithful to fulfill his promise to provide a Savior, and God will be faithful to fulfill all his promises to you and me today. The birth of Jesus is God's promise fulfilled and a reminder that God's promises are guaranteed!

Every page of this book was written with you in mind. You were not only thought of, but you were also prayed for as it was put together. The goal of this book is to help you approach Christmas with ever-deepening enjoyment and an ever-increasing exaltation of Jesus.

I pray this devotional will be a blessing to you.

FOR HIS GLORY,
David Platt

Inasmuch as many have undertaken to compile
a narrative of the things that have been
accomplished among us, just as those who from
the beginning were eyewitnesses and ministers
of the word have delivered them to us, it seemed
good to me also, having followed all things
closely for some time past, to write an orderly
account for you, most excellent Theophilus, that
you may have certainty concerning the things
you have been taught.

THE OLD TESTAMENT BEGINS by telling us that God created mankind in his own likeness. Sadly, the first man and woman failed to obey their Creator. Sinful people formed sinful families, and then sinful families gathered to form sinful nations. One nation in particular enjoyed a special relationship with God, but they also couldn't escape sin. The Israelites, God's chosen people, lived in a repetitive cycle of aiming for obedience yet running after sin. They could not—and, often, would not—live righteous lives.

How would this problem of sin be fixed? From the very beginning, God promised a Deliverer who would save his people from their sin. The Israelites longed for this promised Messiah, thus the Old Testament is full of expectation. When would the Messiah come to restore Israel's relationship with their God? Over hundreds of years, God sent prophets, priests, and kings to lead his people and encourage them as they waited for the Promised One.

At the end of the historical events of the Old Testament, the people of Israel experienced 400 years of silence. Think about that! After centuries of more or less unbroken communication, God's people heard nothing from him for 400 years. No new Scripture, no new prophets—only deafening silence.

But then something changed. Actually, everything changed. After 400 years of silence—and probably 400 years of growing uncertainty—God kept his promise. The Messiah was born. And so, Luke wrote his gospel so that we would have certainty about these things that we have been taught.

Today, many of us feel seasons of uncertainty. We often come into the Christmas season tired, anxious, afraid, and unsure. Can you relate? If so, let this story bring you rest. The Holy Spirit inspired Luke to write this orderly account so that we can be certain about the most important event in the history of world: the Son of God has come to save sinners like us.

The Christmas story shows that God keeps his promises. Believing in the promised Messiah is what leads to true and lasting peace, comfort, and joy.

PROMISES FOR HIS PEOPLE

God is with me wherever I go
(Joshua 1:9).

God will keep me in perfect peace
if my mind is "stayed" on him
(Isaiah 26:3).

God cares for the birds, and he
promises to care for me too
(Matthew 6:26).

The Lord is with me always, to the
end of time (Matthew 28:20).

If I abide in the Lord and his words
abide in me, whatever I ask will be
given to me (John 15:7).

I am justified by his free grace
(Romans 3:24).

I have peace with God because
I've been justified by faith in Jesus
(Romans 5:1).

I have access to God's grace
(Romans 5:2).

There is no condemnation for
me because I am in Christ Jesus
(Romans 8:1).

The Holy Spirit will help me to pray
(Romans 8:26–27).

All things work together for my
good (Romans 8:28).

Nothing will separate me from the
love of Christ (Romans 8:35).

I shall bear the likeness (and
resurrection body) of Jesus, the
"man of heaven" (1 Corinthians
15:49).

My labor in the Lord is not in vain
(1 Corinthians 15:58).

I am being transformed into God's
likeness (2 Corinthians 3:18).

God comforts me when I'm sad
(2 Corinthians 7:6).

God blesses me so I can do good
works (2 Corinthians 9:8).

God's grace is sufficient for me
(2 Corinthians 12:9).

The Holy Spirit in me guarantees
my inheritance in Christ (Ephesians
1:11–14).

God has created good works for
me to walk in today (Ephesians
2:10).

I have been brought into the
body of Christ by his own blood
(Ephesians 2:13).

In Christ I can approach God
with freedom and confidence
(Ephesians 3:11–12).

God will supply all my needs
(Philippians 4:19).

The Father has qualified me to
share in the inheritance of his
people (Colossians 1:12).

Christ lives in me (Colossians 1:27).

Because God is faithful, he
will make me holy—like he is
(1 Thessalonians 5:23–24).

God is just; he will repay with
trouble those who trouble me
(2 Thessalonians 1:6).

God has given me a spirit of
power, love, and self-discipline
(2 Timothy 1:7).

I have a crown of righteousness
awaiting me, because I long for his
appearing (2 Timothy 4:8).

God won't lie to me, because God
cannot lie (Titus 1:2).

Jesus will help me when I'm
tempted (Hebrews 2:18).

God will never leave me or forsake
me (Hebrews 13:5).

God uses hard times to make
me more mature in him (James
1:2–4).

If I ask for wisdom from God, he
will give it to me (James 1:5).

If I resist the devil, he will run from
me (James 4:7).

If I draw near to God, he will draw
near to me (James 4:8).

My prayers are powerful (James
5:16).

He cares for me (1 Peter 5:7).

In my sufferings, God will
strengthen, confirm, and establish
me (1 Peter 5:10).

A new heaven and earth await me
(2 Peter 3:13).

He forgives and cleanses me as
I confess my sins to him (1 John
1:9).

When Jesus reappears, I'll be made
like him (1 John 3:2).

God has given me eternal life in
his Son (1 John 5:11).

02

HAVE YOU EVER READ the word righteous and wondered what it meant? It's definitely one of those "Christianese" words. It's used throughout the Bible, and the word often shows up in praise songs. But we rarely use it in every-day conversation.

In the Bible, only a handful of people are described as righteous. Notice that righteous doesn't mean sinless or perfect. The person who is righteous is the one who trusts God and walks with him faithfully. So, when Luke describes Zechariah and Elizabeth as righteous, he's saying they trusted and obeyed God. They were living examples of how God designed us all to live in relationship with him.

The last sentence in today's passage, however, carries within it a hard truth for all of us: even righteous people who walk blamelessly before God have strug-gles. Why would God allow hardship for some of the few people who actually trust and obey him? Did Zechariah and Elizabeth ask this same question? Take a moment and imagine what it would be like to long for and pray for a child but be unable to have one. Perhaps this couple saw other people around them get preg-nant multiple times and grow their families, while they themselves pleaded with the Lord and got no response as they continued to get older and older.

The amazing thing is that despite the sadness and grief Zechariah and Eliz-abeth may have felt, they continued to trust and obey God. For them, God was not reduced to a gift giver; God's presence was the gift itself. His commandments were for their joy, and every good gift he chose to give were a reflection of his goodness. Zechariah and Elizabeth trusted God's promises and purposes.

As we continue to read this story, we see that God did, in fact, give Elizabeth a child—one who would prepare the way for Jesus. God's timing and plan are always better than ours. When we are struggling and don't understand what God is doing, we can trust his power, his character, and his track record. God makes the impossible possible for his glory and our joy.

In the days of Herod, king of Judea, there was a priest named Zechariah, of the division of Abijah. And he had a wife from the daughters of Aaron, and her name was Elizabeth. And they were both righteous before God, walking blamelessly in all the commandments and statutes of the Lord. But they had no child, because Elizabeth was barren, and both were advanced in years.

Now while he was serving as priest before God when his division was on duty, according to the custom of the priesthood, he was chosen by lot to enter the temple of the Lord and burn incense. And the whole multitude of the people were praying outside at the hour of incense. And there appeared to him an angel of the Lord standing on the right side of the altar of incense. And Zechariah was troubled when he saw him, and fear fell upon him. But the angel said to him, "Do not be afraid, Zechariah, for your prayer has been heard, and your wife Elizabeth will bear you a son, and you shall call his name John. And you will have joy and gladness, and many will rejoice at his birth, for he will be great before the Lord. And he must not drink wine or strong drink, and he will be filled with the Holy Spirit, even from his mother's womb."

03

HOW LONG had Elizabeth and Zechariah begged God for a child? How many times had they pleaded with God to do for them what they couldn't do for themselves? Luke doesn't include those details, but we can assume it was a long time based on the fact that they were, "advanced in years" (Luke 1:7), which is a polite way of saying they were old.

Perhaps you've prayed about something for years—a prodigal child, a longing for a spouse, health problems, a desire to have children, a job change, financial difficulties, mental health issues—and it seems that heaven is silent. You've yet to see the fulfillment of your prayers in the way you'd hoped. If this is you, let the angel's words to Zechariah be a balm to your weary soul: "Your prayer has been heard" (Luke 1:13).

We're all familiar with Paul's words in Romans 8:28: "And we know that for those who love God all things work together for good, for those who are called according to his purpose." If we truly believe those words, not just as a warm and fuzzy memory verse but as bedrock reality, then we know that when God does not give us what we long for, we know it's for our lasting good and his ultimate glory.

God hears his children and wants us to persist in prayer just like Elizabeth and Zechariah. So, keep on asking, keep on seeking, and keep on knocking, because God knows what you need and when you need it. What's more, he is doing something in your own heart through persistence and patience. He is conforming you into the image of Jesus.

As John Piper beautifully reminds us, "God is often masterminding a thousand details behind the tapestry of our lives, and we only get to see three of them. Sometimes we see them immediately. Sometimes we don't for years. Sometimes we don't see them until we're with Him in eternity. And yet the truth remains: He is still in the business of answering our prayers."

CHRISTMAS CATEGORIES

Choose a letter, then think of words that fit the categories below that begin with your letter. Want to make it harder? Set a timer, and race to beat it!

1 A Christmas song

----

2 Something you eat around Christmas

----

3 A Christmas tradition

----

4 A person, place, or thing in the Bible's account of Jesus's birth

----

5 A Christmas movie

----

6 Something green

----

7 Something red

----

8 A common Christmas present

----

9 A Christmas activity

----

10 A Christmas decoration

READ
LUKE 1:16 – 17

And he will turn many of the children of Israel to the Lord their God, and he will go before him in the spirit and power of Elijah, to turn the hearts of the fathers to the children, and the disobedient to the wisdom of the just, to make ready for the Lord a people prepared.

04

IF YOU FEEL STRONGLY about something, it doesn't mean you always will. You might have had a strong belief that animals belong outdoors until a pet enters your family and you find yourself willingly sharing your home and maybe even your bed with a furry friend. More significantly, maybe you had strong feelings about not wanting children but now you find yourself desiring a family. We can be passionate about something only to find ourselves feeling differently about it later. We change our minds. That's a natural part of being human.

But what about changing our heart? Is that so natural? No, that work is supernatural. It's a work of the Lord. Thankfully, it's a work he is committed to.

As you read the passage today, consider the different ways the Lord has changed your heart. Recall how you once pursued things you thought would bring meaning to your life, but how now you know those things are futile. Consider how reading God's Word or spending the weekend worshiping and serving in the church at one time was an inconvenience, but now it's a blessing to your soul. Maybe you used to be diligent to keep areas of your life hidden, but now you're vulnerable and welcome godly accountability. If these things are true of you, the Lord has changed your heart.

As God's child, you should be eager to share with others how God changed your life when he turned your heart to him. Who might you share that with today? Take some time to pray for one person you can share this with.

If you are reading this and you know your heart is not turned toward the Lord, then today can be the day that changes. God has a plan for you. Pray and ask him to turn your heart to him.

05

"HE LOOKED ON ME." Consider what that phrase meant for Elizabeth and everyone after her who experiences the same. God looked on her. The Most High God set his gaze on Elizabeth to take away her disgrace.

In many cultures, infertility brings intense shame and suffering. To be labeled infertile in Elizabeth's culture would mean she likely experienced economic deprivation, social isolation, and loss of community status. Just imagine: an intense, personal pain turns into a hurtful, social stigma with devastating consequences.

We all know the feeling of shame. And we all know the temptation to hide in response. We don't want to be seen or known because if we are, we'd surely be rejected. Shame creeps in when you're called names at school or when you don't make the team, when you've failed at an important task or when you're cheated on by a spouse. We feel shame when someone takes advantage of us and we're powerless to do anything about it, when someone convinces you that you're unlovable or a nobody. Those feelings in this broken world can be crushing. What in your life leads you to feel shame? What facts about your life do you fear would cause others to reject you?

What if there were someone who knew every detail about you and would never ever reject you? That's the kind of acceptance God had for Elizabeth when he looked on her, and that's the kind of acceptance God has for us in Christ Jesus. Only in the gospel can we be fully known and fully loved. Restored, not rejected.

Notice how Elizabeth responds to the Lord's acceptance in the last sentence of today's passage (verse 25). God has transformed her shame-ridden identity into one marked by great honor. What an exchange! That same exchange is true for all of us who trust in Christ. On the cross, he took the full weight of our sin and shame (Isaiah 53:4–6). And when we come to Jesus by faith, he looks on us and takes away our reproach. He sees the real us and washes away our sin so we can have a relationship with him and be with him for all eternity.

And Zechariah said to the angel, "How shall I know this? For I am an old man, and my wife is advanced in years." And the angel answered him, "I am Gabriel. I stand in the presence of God, and I was sent to speak to you and to bring you this good news. And behold, you will be silent and unable to speak until the day that these things take place, because you did not believe my words, which will be fulfilled in their time." And the people were waiting for Zechariah, and they were wondering at his delay in the temple. And when he came out, he was unable to speak to them, and they realized that he had seen a vision in the temple. And he kept making signs to them and remained mute. And when his time of service was ended, he went to his home. After these days his wife Elizabeth conceived, and for five months she kept herself hidden, saying, "Thus the Lord has done for me in the days when he looked on me, to take away my reproach among people."

EYE SPY

Can you find all of the Christmas symbols? Grab a pen and check them off as you go!

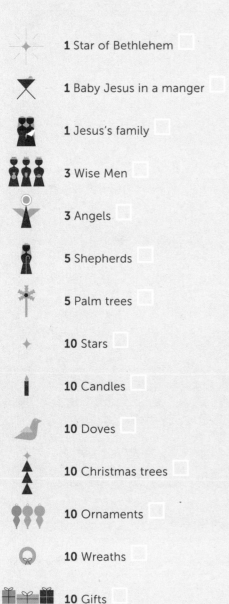

1 Star of Bethlehem ☐

1 Baby Jesus in a manger ☐

1 Jesus's family ☐

3 Wise Men ☐

3 Angels ☐

5 Shepherds ☐

5 Palm trees ☐

10 Stars ☐

10 Candles ☐

10 Doves ☐

10 Christmas trees ☐

10 Ornaments ☐

10 Wreaths ☐

10 Gifts ☐

In the sixth month the angel Gabriel was sent from God to a city of Galilee named Nazareth, to a virgin betrothed to a man whose name was Joseph, of the house of David. And the virgin's name was Mary. And he came to her and said, "Greetings, O favored one, the Lord is with you!" But she was greatly troubled at the saying, and tried to discern what sort of greeting this might be. And the angel said to her, "Do not be afraid, Mary, for you have found favor with God. And behold, you will conceive in your womb and bear a son, and you shall call his name Jesus. He will be great and will be called the Son of the Most High. And the Lord God will give to him the throne of his father David, and he will reign over the house of Jacob forever, and of his kingdom there will be no end."

06

THIS IS THE REASON we celebrate Christmas every year, and this is where the story of Scripture begins to shift. Remember what we learned on Day 1? We learned how God made people, how the first people chose not to trust God, and how their relationship with God was broken. The world was not as it should be, but God promised to come back and fix what was broken. God's people waited, and watched, and prayed. People continued to disobey God, and God continued to rescue people from their broken world. And then, there were 400 years of silence.

It's in today's passage that Mary finds out that God is finally coming back to fix what was broken through her giving birth to his Son. Let's focus on a few phrases from the last two sentences of the angel's announcement.

"Son of the Most High."
Most High was a title for God. Mary and other Jews would have been familiar with that title because it's used throughout the Old Testament. So when Mary hears the angel identify Jesus as the "Son of the Most High," she understood what that meant. Her Son would be unique in that he would have the same essence as the Most High God.

"The throne of his father David, and he will reign over the house of Jacob forever."
Jesus would also be a son of David. The angel told Mary that Jesus was the one everyone had been waiting for—the fulfillment of all the prophecies and promises. The Old Testament prophesied that a descendant from both David and Jacob would defeat their enemy and rule over God's people. Jesus would be the "King of the Jews."

"Of his kingdom there will be no end."
Not only was he the one everyone waited for, his arrival meant there would be no more waiting ever again. He would restore his people forever. Unlike previous kings, his regime would not have an expiration date.

This is why the story shifts. Jesus, God's Son, who was promised to us back when our relationship with God was broken, has finally come to restore us to himself, now and forever. As followers of Jesus, we celebrate his rescue of us not once a year, but every day. We are walking, living, breathing, redeemed children, and we get to tell others all that he has done for us!

07

IN LUKE 1:18 (Day 5) we saw Zechariah's response to the angel's message. He doubted that his aging, barren wife would have a son. His question revealed his unbelief. That's why the angel exposes Zechariah and takes away his ability to speak.

Yesterday, we read about another angelic visit, but not at the altar and not to a priest. This time, the angel appears in the small town of Nazareth to a teenager named Mary, and gives her similar news to Zechariah's—an unexpected baby is on the way.

To this shocking news, Mary, like Zechariah, asks a question: "How will this be, since I am a virgin?" But she doesn't ask out of unbelief but amazement. She—a virgin!—was to carry the Son of God in her womb, and she felt unworthy. Tomorrow, we will learn more about how Mary's response reflects her humble heart. But for today, consider simply that our questions to God don't always stem from unbelief.

Mary had questions, but she also had faith. The two are not opposed to one another.

Have there been times when you had questions for God? When have you, like Mary, asked the Lord, "How will this be?" When we bring our questions to God while still believing he is the Sovereign Lord, we can ask without fear. He does not judge us when we don't understand.

So bring your questions to God. Share your doubts with him. Your questions may actually reveal your faith as you ask with a heart of humility and trust.

READ
LUKE 1:34

And Mary
said to
the angel,
"How will
this be,
since I
am a
virgin?"

And the angel answered her, "The Holy Spirit will come upon you, and the power of the Most High will overshadow you; therefore the child to be born will be called holy—the Son of God. And behold, your relative Elizabeth in her old age has also conceived a son, and this is the sixth month with her who was called barren."

THE ANGEL OF THE LORD answered Mary's question about how she, a virgin, could have a child. He explained that the Holy Spirit himself would come upon her and she would have a child who would be called holy, the Son of God.

As a young Jewish woman, Mary would have been taught that God had promised a Deliverer. But an angel of the Lord tells Mary that she will bear the child.

However, God doesn't only provide an answer to Mary's question. He also reveals an extraordinary yet personal plan to care for her during this season. Mary learns that she does not have to walk through her unexpected pregnancy alone. You see, God also had an extraordinary plan for Mary's cousin Elizabeth, who carried in her womb the baby who would grow up to prepare the way for her Son, the promised Messiah.

Neither of these women expected this plan for their lives. Yet they trusted in their caring God to provide according to his good timing and his good plan.

Just as with Mary and Elizabeth, God has a plan for each of us that intersects with his plan for others in God's family. As we faithfully walk with God according to his plan for our life, we encourage others who also are walking with God according to his plan for their lives.

This Christmas season, pause to consider those whom God has brought around you. Consider your family, your friends, and your community, and know that your faithful obedience to Jesus and his plan for your life should affect them in some way. Be encouraged that you, too, are an important part of God's unfolding plan to take the good news of Jesus Christ to those around you, and to the world.

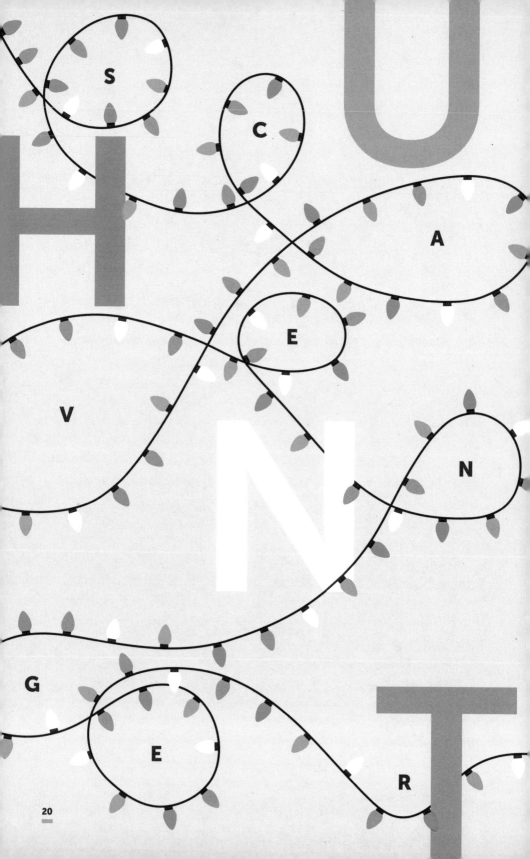

SCAVENGER HUNT

Don't forget to get photo or video evidence!

5 POINTS

Find a red tree decoration

Find Christmas lights

Find two bells

Find a Christmas card

Find a candy cane

15 POINTS

Whistle, hum or sing the melody of any Christmas song

Give someone a Christmas gift

Do an act of service in your house, neighborhood, or work that would bless someone else

10 POINTS

Pretend to be an animal that may have been in the stable where Jesus was born

Write your own Christmas joke

Text or tell someone you love them

20 POINTS

Sing a Christmas carol

Invite someone to join you for a Christmas Eve gathering

Recite Luke 2:10–11 from memory

TOTAL POINTS

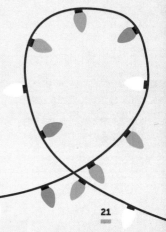

09

TRY THIS. Stand up and lift your right foot off the ground and begin circling it in a clockwise direction. While you continue moving your foot in circles, draw a six with your finger in the air two times. Did your foot change direction? For most people it is impossible for their foot to be moving clockwise while their finger moves counterclockwise, which happens when you draw the number six. Was that true for you?

Here's another experiment. Stick out your tongue and try to touch it to your nose. Can you do it? Ask a friend or family member to try. Can they do it?

These are silly things that are nearly impossible to do. They make us laugh as we try them. But there are other things that are impossible, but not silly at all. There are some things we just cannot do.

When you face impossible things, it can bring up many difficult questions. What will happen if we can't make ends meet? What will happen if my wayward child never comes back to the Lord? What will happen if I am always alone? What will happen if my friend or family member never comes to know Jesus? These questions can tempt us to hopelessness. But hopelessness comes when we are preoccupied with the impossible situation rather than with the God for whom nothing is impossible. Our God isn't limited by any situation.

Mary heard seemingly impossible news, but the angel reminded her of a crucial truth: "Nothing will be impossible with God."

We all need this reminder at various times—no, not when we're trying to touch our nose with our tongue, but when God's promises seem impossible and unbelievable. When your situation feels beyond repair, when a heart seems as cold as ice, when you can't imagine things turning around, remember what the angel told Mary: "Nothing will be impossible with God." Whatever God has promised, will happen. Even if his plans are not what we expect, he works all things for our good and his glory (Romans 8:28). Trust him, even in impossible situations.

✦

"For nothing

will be impossible

with God."

And Mary said,

"Behold, I am the

servant of the Lord;

let it be to me according

to your word."

And the angel departed

from her.

10

FOR THE SECOND TIME in Luke's first chapter, a birth is foretold. In verse 13, we read about the angel Gabriel telling Zechariah that his wife Elizabeth would give birth to a son named John. Then in verse 31, we read about the angel Gabriel telling Mary that she would conceive and bear a Son, and his name would be Jesus.

We see two very similar situations with two very different responses. Two of God's people are understandably afraid at seeing an angel who brings news of an unexpected pregnancy.

Think for a moment about the contrast between Mary and Zechariah. Zechariah is an elderly man, and Mary, a teenage girl. Mary lives in the despised region of Galilee, in Nazareth, an insignificant village. She is a nobody from nowhere. Zechariah is a priest in the temple, constantly surrounded by visible signs of the living God. He is a somebody from somewhere. Yet still, in the most magnificent turn of events, Mary demonstrates a simple faith—and Zechariah struggles.

Zechariah is a righteous man who loves God's Word, yet he struggles to believe God's words through the angel. Mary hears the word of God and believes something even more astonishing: that she, a virgin, will conceive. Mary's reply to the angel in today's verse is the language of great faith and humility.

Mary's example can help us to reflect on the nature of true faith. Mary believes what God speaks before she can see the evidence of it in her own life. Faith by its very nature is not the same as sight and as followers of Jesus we live by faith and not by sight. The Bible teaches us not to expect, in the normal Christian life, the kind of angelic visit that Mary experienced. But we nonetheless have the same task: to believe the words God has spoken to us through his Word. This Christmas season, may we marvel at the beauty of Mary's faith and ask God to give us a faith like hers.

11

RIGHT AFTER MARY LEARNS she is pregnant with the promised Savior of the world, she travels to see her relative Elizabeth who also is pregnant. As Elizabeth hears Mary's voice, the baby inside Elizabeth's womb leaps! Then, filled with the Holy Spirit, she calls Mary the "mother of my Lord."

Did you catch that? It's so easy to read through God's Word and miss little details. What happened after Elizabeth was filled with the Holy Spirit? She proclaims that the baby inside Mary is the Lord, that is, the One whom the Scriptures had promised since the beginning of humankind (Genesis 3), back when the first sin separated us from God. Who told her this information? The Holy Spirit!

Who is the Holy Spirit? The Holy Spirit is the third person of the Trinity. To make it really simple, the Holy Spirit is God. In the first book of the Bible, God promises to come back and fix what we broke. In today's passage, God tells Elizabeth that the time has come to fulfill that promise through the Lord in Mary's womb.

Followers of Jesus today have the same Holy Spirit living in them. The Spirit who revealed to Elizabeth the identity of the Messiah is the same Spirit who later raises Jesus from the dead (Romans 8:11). If you're a follower of Jesus, then the Holy Spirit lives in you also.

You may have heard the Christmas story countless times. You may have celebrated this holiday longer than you can remember. But never grow tired of the truth that God's Spirit lives inside you. You can do more than go through the motions of your own traditions. You can marvel in awe at God's power and love each time you hear the same story.

In those days Mary arose and went with haste into the hill country, to a town in Judah, and she entered the house of Zechariah and greeted Elizabeth. And when Elizabeth heard the greeting of Mary, the baby leaped in her womb. And Elizabeth was filled with the Holy Spirit, and she exclaimed with a loud cry, "Blessed are you among women, and blessed is the fruit of your womb! And why is this granted to me that the mother of my Lord should come to me? For behold, when the sound of your greeting came to my ears, the baby in my womb leaped for joy."

AD-LIB FUN

Fill out the words on the trees and then transcribe them into the story on the right. Read aloud for a sweet (or silly) Christmas story!

1

_____
adjective

10

_____
verb-ing

2

_____
verb

5

_____
plural noun

11

_____
adjective

3

_____
adjective

6

_____
plural animal

8

_____
color

12

_____
adjective

4

_____
verb

7

_____
color

9

_____
plural noun

13

_____
person/people

There are many ways to celebrate Christmas that

make _____ memories that last a lifetime.
                1

You can _____ _____
                2   3

ornaments to _____ on the tree.
                      4

Baking cookies shaped like _____
                                         5

or _____, and decorating them
            6

with _____ and _____
              7   8

_____ is a tasty way to celebrate with
          9

friends and family. Finding the perfect gift and

_____ it in _____ paper
          10   11

with a _____ bow on top is a great way
                  12

to be generous during Christmas. But my favorite

way to celebrate Christmas is going to church with

_____ on Christmas Eve, and
          13

singing _____ and
                  14

_____ with my church family.
          15

12

THE WORD "BLESSED" in this passage is sometimes translated "happy." The Lord spoke to Mary, she believed what he said, and she was truly happy—she was "blessed."

Do you long for lasting happiness? Do you long for the deep contentment and satisfaction that can be found in walking with God even on really hard days? If you want to be blessed, what should you do? Believe the Lord when he speaks.

The Old Testament is filled with priests and prophets who bring messages from God to his people. But what about today? Do you ever wonder if the Lord still speaks to his people?

Today, God speaks to his people through his Word. The original authors wrote the Bible under the inspiration of the Holy Spirit. That means that when we read God's Word, we are hearing God "speak"!

We should take comfort in what we read because God's words are sure and trustworthy. He always keeps his promises, and what he says will indeed come to pass. Like Mary, if you want to be blessed, take God at his word. You might begin by meditating on these promises from God:

God is near to his people.
(See Psalm 119:151; 145:18; Romans 8:11; James 4:8.)

God forgives the sins of those who repent and believe.
(See Isaiah 43:25; Acts 10:43; Romans 10:9.)

God brings comfort and peace to those who are in Christ.
(See Psalm 119:76; Matthew 11:28–29; 2 Corinthians 1:3–4.)

"And blessed

is she who believed

that there would be

a fulfillment of what

was spoken to her

from the Lord."

13

WHY ME? Have you ever asked yourself that question? We usually ask it with a sigh of discouragement when something disappointing happens to us. But this question can be asked with a completely different motivation. It can be asked from a heart of humility and gratitude. When you receive kindness that you don't deserve or when you are shown unmerited favor you can find yourself asking, Why me? This kind of question might have crossed Mary's mind when she was told she would be the mother of the Messiah.

Mary was an ordinary girl with a heart deeply devoted to knowing her God. Her song of praise overflows with her knowledge of him. Did you notice how little of the song is about herself? Instead, she sings about her great God and how he cares for his children from generation to generation. She wasn't an amazing leader or a charismatic pillar among believers. She was a girl who loved God—and he saw her devotion and faith. He looked on her lowly estate.

God sees you, too. You don't have to write a book, preach a sermon, lead a movement, or make a significant contribution to some special cause to be seen by God. He sees the faith of all who humbly trust and obey him. He sees and he shows himself to be a merciful God who is kind to his children.

Have you experienced the blessing and grace of God in your life? Has God's goodness surprised you in ways that made you ask, Why me? Take some time to write out a personal song of praise to God (on the following page) in response to the ways he has blessed you. Let Mary's song inspire you. Your song doesn't have to be poetic or artistic. Let it simply be an overflow of your gratitude that he sees you as you seek to follow him day-by-day.

And Mary said, "My soul magnifies the Lord, and my spirit rejoices in God my Savior, for he has looked on the humble estate of his servant. For behold, from now on all generations will call me blessed; for he who is mighty has done great things for me, and holy is his name. And his mercy is for those who fear him from generation to generation. He has shown strength with his arm; he has scattered the proud in the thoughts of their hearts; he has brought down the mighty from their thrones and exalted those of humble estate; he has filled the hungry with good things, and the rich he has sent away empty. He has helped his servant Israel, in remembrance of his mercy, as he spoke to our fathers, to Abraham and to his offspring forever." And Mary remained with her about three months and returned to her home.

MY PERSONAL SONG OF PRAISE

Read the devotion from Day 13. Then write out your personal song of praise in response to the ways God has blessed you.

_____

_____

_____

_____

_____

_____

_____

_____

_____

_____

_____

_____

_____

SCRAMBLE

To the right are six words found in the song "Joy to the World"—but they are all jumbled! Unscramble each of these words, one letter to each square and then, unscramble the circled letters to form a new word that fills in the blank in the answer at the bottom of the page.

"Joy to the World" was named the most-published Christmas hymn in North America in the late '90s. The lyrics were written by English writer Isaac Watts, who based them on the second half of Psalm 98. Rather than celebrating the birth of Christ, the text of this hymn represents Christ's triumphant

___ ___ ___ ___ ___

RTHUT

HRATE

GIUDNNOS

OSIRLEG

VAEHNE

ERPATE

ANSWER

14

AS WE APPROACH THE END of Luke 1, we come to the birth of John. The story is simple and yet beautifully profound.

When we first read these verses, it may seem like we're reading a story about Zechariah and the instantaneous miracle of him regaining the ability to speak. Or maybe this is a story about Elizabeth and the miracle of giving birth in her old age. One could even say this is a story about John and the great significance of his life and ministry. But, ultimately, this is a story first and foremost about God. He is the main character in this drama, and Luke wants us to see in vivid detail the hand of the Lord. Everything in the story of John the Baptist is evidence of the mighty intervention of God, which is why Luke ends this passage with the comment: "For the hand of the Lord was with him" (vs. 66).

We saw the hand of God when the angel Gabriel told Zechariah that he would have a son. We saw the hand of God when an elderly, barren couple miraculously has their first child. We see the hand of God when Zechariah is made deaf and mute as judgment for his unbelief. And again, we see the hand of God when Zechariah's tongue is loosed and he begins to bless God. The hand of God is everywhere in these verses and Luke doesn't want us to miss it.

The same can be said for all of Scripture. Psalm 19:7 calls the Bible the "testimony" of the Lord. Scripture is how God reveals himself to us. So as we approach Scripture, let us look for the hand of God. Every passage declares something about him, and pursuing knowledge of him is a rich endeavor that carries with it a great reward.

Now the time came for Elizabeth to give birth, and she bore a son. And her neighbors and relatives heard that the Lord had shown great mercy to her, and they rejoiced with her. And on the eighth day they came to circumcise the child. And they would have called him Zechariah after his father, but his mother answered, "No; he shall be called John." And they said to her, "None of your relatives is called by this name." And they made signs to his father, inquiring what he wanted him to be called. And he asked for a writing tablet and wrote, "His name is John." And they all wondered. And immediately his mouth was opened and his tongue loosed, and he spoke, blessing God. And fear came on all their neighbors. And all these things were talked about through all the hill country of Judea, and all who heard them laid them up in their hearts, saying, "What then will this child be?" For the hand of the Lord was with him.

And his father Zechariah was filled with the Holy Spirit and prophesied, saying, "Blessed be the Lord God of Israel, for he has visited and redeemed his people and has raised up a horn of salvation for us in the house of his servant David, as he spoke by the mouth of his holy prophets from of old, that we should be saved from our enemies and from the hand of all who hate us; to show the mercy promised to our fathers and to remember his holy covenant, the oath that he swore to our father Abraham, to grant us that we, being delivered from the hand of our enemies, might serve him without fear, in holiness and righteousness before him all our days."

NOTICE THE CHANGE in Zechariah. Remember, Zechariah was the priest who was unable to speak because he didn't believe God's message. Now we see a completely different picture. This once-silent priest is now filled with the Holy Spirit and can't help but speak! He prophesies that God's covenant to Abraham so long ago is now being fulfilled. Zechariah's uncertainty is gone. The man who once questioned God now boldly declares God's faithfulness to David and David's household. Salvation has come!

Zechariah blesses God for visiting his people. God didn't send just any strong leader to save those he loves. Instead, God himself came in the flesh. God personally visited his people to redeem them. Zechariah praises God because he raised up a Savior. The Israelites were hopeless on their own. Now God sends a Savior to keep his promise to their forefathers to show them mercy.

Filled with the Holy Spirit, Zechariah rightly acknowledges what God has done. He then proclaims that this mighty work of God demands a response from God's followers. Let's not miss that! God's people have been delivered, which means that we who were once afraid of him can now serve him without fear, in holiness and righteousness all of our days. This ability has been "granted" to us.

What would it look like for you personally to serve God without fear? Are there areas where you should serve him more courageously? Do you have gifts that you can use in your local church? Are there people in your community who could use a helping hand? What would it look like for you to take a step of faith in service this Christmas season? If we have been saved, we can serve the Lord in holiness and righteousness.

So let's remember that our salvation is based on the righteousness of Christ alone. Therefore, we have nothing to fear. We can boldly serve our holy God with clean hands and clean hearts.

16

ON AN ORDINARY DAY in Thailand in 2018, twelve boys from a soccer team and their coach were enjoying a day together when a torrential rain caused them to flee to a nearby cave for shelter. The water forced them further back; they desperately searched for dry ground and couldn't find it. Eventually, they got trapped in the depths of the cave in complete darkness. Minutes turned into hours and hours turned into days as they waited for the water to subside. But the rain outside continued. As the days went on, the boys' perilous situation left most thinking that there was no way for them to survive. Until, against all odds, rescue divers found them alive. Certainly, there were times when they despaired. But the day the rescue diver's light broke through the water at the base of the pitch-black cavity where the team had taken refuge, hope returned to their hearts.

The utter darkness of the cave confused the boys. After their rescue, many of the boys immediately wanted to know how long they had been down there. Darkness not only steals our ability to see, but it also deprives us of accurate knowledge about our lives. Outside of a relationship with God, our lives don't make sense. Trials disorient us, our sins entrap us, and we are left without hope. Who or what can pierce this spiritual darkness? Only the Lord.

Though you may never have been trapped in a cave, all of humanity has a similar story. For hundreds of years, the world was like the boys in the cave— full of people sitting in darkness and only marginally aware that death was just around the corner. But God was on a rescue mission and sent a messenger to prepare the way. Like the rescue divers, a messenger of hope would proclaim that the Messiah had come. And his coming meant that there was now a way out of the darkness.

If you know Jesus, you have been rescued. What's more, you must share the message of hope with those who remain in darkness. Who in your life needs this message? Consider inviting them to attend a Christmas service with you.

"And you, child, will be called the prophet of the Most High; for you will go before the Lord to prepare his ways, to give knowledge of salvation to his people in the forgiveness of their sins, because of the tender mercy of our God, whereby the sunrise shall visit us from on high to give light to those who sit in darkness and in the shadow of death, to guide our feet into the way of peace." And the child grew and became strong in spirit, and he was in the wilderness until the day of his public appearance to Israel.

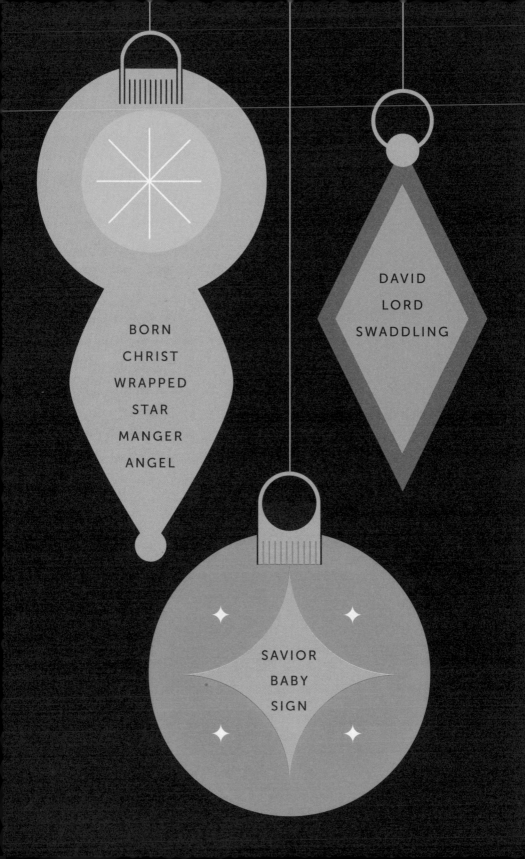

BORN
CHRIST
WRAPPED
STAR
MANGER
ANGEL

DAVID
LORD
SWADDLING

SAVIOR
BABY
SIGN

WORD SEARCH

```
Y  Z  F  C  H  X  X  A  J  B  E  V  E  S  Y
C  S  Z  J  H  N  S  N  M  H  Y  X  U  I  R
H  V  H  W  D  R  O  G  H  Y  J  G  E  G  O
F  E  U  T  J  O  I  E  O  D  G  W  E  N  I
J  R  S  R  L  B  S  S  T  Q  H  R  E  H  V
H  G  E  W  E  F  I  B  T  H  Z  A  Q  O  A
N  A  L  G  M  I  C  V  A  G  D  P  I  U  S
X  H  E  U  N  G  K  H  D  B  V  P  J  H  D
B  V  G  T  D  A  R  Z  X  F  Y  E  X  L  V
U  S  N  C  O  I  M  F  R  U  H  D  A  T  U
N  J  A  K  T  T  V  E  M  C  B  Q  N  Y  T
L  N  L  D  Z  V  G  A  S  U  H  T  B  X  T
C  G  R  N  U  S  W  A  D  D  L  I  N  G  L
S  O  V  Y  A  G  P  W  D  B  M  S  G  U  H
L  H  N  M  B  S  T  A  R  O  F  M  D  V  D
```

17

LUKE WAS A DOCTOR (see Col. 4:14). He devoted years of his life to studying and training for the medical profession. Given this background, you might expect more detail in his retelling of the birth of Jesus. However, Luke recounts the story with a simple sentence, "She gave birth to her firstborn son"—simple, but intriguing, words.

What was Mary thinking? How did two young people manage the birth of a child with no support system? Did Joseph lift voiceless prayers to heaven while holding Mary's hand through a long night of labor? We don't know any of that information.

A good writer knows that vivid descriptions can greatly improve writing but going overboard on detail can slow down a narrative and overwhelm the reader. It's here that we must remind ourselves that the point of these verses is not the physical birth of Jesus but rather the astounding fact that the Lord of heaven came to live on Earth in human flesh. The Creator of the universe entered the world as a helpless baby. One silent night—on a night just like any other in Israel, with no pomp or celebration from anyone—a child unlike any other was born. This child was the Lord Jesus Christ.

These verses record the single most important moment in all of history. "The Word became flesh and dwelt among us" (John 1:14). In God's goodness, he sent Jesus to ransom us from the power of sin and make us ready to be with him, both now and forever. This is the good news of Christmas, and the reason the name of Jesus is the name above all names.

In those days a decree went out from Caesar Augustus that all the world should be registered. This was the first registration when Quirinius was governor of Syria. And all went to be registered, each to his own town. And Joseph also went up from Galilee, from the town of Nazareth, to Judea, to the city of David, which is called Bethlehem, because he was of the house and lineage of David, to be registered with Mary, his betrothed, who was with child. And while they were there, the time came for her to give birth. And she gave birth to her firstborn son and wrapped him in swaddling cloths and laid him in a manger, because there was no place for them in the inn.

And in the same region there were shepherds
out in the field, keeping watch over their flock
by night. And an angel of the Lord appeared to
them, and the glory of the Lord shone around
them, and they were filled with great fear.

18

HAVE YOU EVER WONDERED why the angels went to the shepherds to proclaim Jesus was born? Why didn't they tell the priest, or the king, or the popular people? In just a few words, we're introduced to the people who first received the message God's people had waited centuries to hear. While we don't know a lot about them, we can reasonably draw a few conclusions based on the culture and practices at that time.

Because these shepherds were out in the field at night, they were likely not landowners who owned the flock, but probably night-shift bondservants or low-paid wage earners who were hired to protect the flock at night. This could have made them unclean, unable to enter the temple, and unable to participate in worship.

According to Jewish law, sheep that were used for the offerings on the Sabbath could be used to atone for sins and reconcile the sinner back to God for a season. They had to be a one-year-old male lamb who had been outside for one year. Generations of shepherds tended these sacred flocks and sometimes risked their lives to keep the animals from going astray. After pouring their lives out into their flocks, the shepherds would separate the lambs, choosing only the perfect firstborn males to take to Jerusalem. There, the lambs would be purchased by those who wished to atone for their sins.

None of this is in Luke's text. So we can't know for sure who these shepherds were. But based on cultural history and extrabiblical Jewish law, we know it's likely they were caring for and protecting lambs reserved for sacrificial atonement. This was the very thing that could restore their relationship back to God, and ironically, they weren't able to do it for themselves because they were unclean.

So why did angels tell these shepherds first? We don't know for certain. And yet, it may have been because these were people who had no hope. If you find yourself in a similar position, know that the Lord sees you and pursues you.

[Spoiler alert] What happened after the shepherds heard the news of Jesus's arrival? A few verses later, we read that they left the sheep to see baby Jesus. They went to see the perfect Lamb of God, Jesus, who would one day provide the atonement they had long been denied.

19

WHAT A SIGNIFICANT and important statement! When we take it to heart, our fear is replaced by joy. This good news is for all people.

We've already talked about the initial recipients of this good news: lowly shepherds. And yet, we see here that this news is for kings and rulers, too. It's for all people—for the Jew and the Gentile, the slave and the free, the rich and the poor, the young and the old. The angel declares good news for the timid and the bold, the sinful and the shameful, the mighty and the weak. The angel brings good news for all people.

Please hear this: that means that the angel brought good news for you, too.

The angel brought good news for your family, your neighbors, your coworkers, your friends, and even your enemies. It's good news for all people everywhere.

Are you experiencing the joy of this good news? If not, what anxieties and stresses weigh heavy on your heart, robbing you of joy this Christmas season?

Rest assured that this good news of great joy is for you. You're invited to worship the Savior just as you are. Come weary. Come lonely. Just come. Take comfort in this news. And don't be afraid. Right now, before jumping back into your busy day, take a few minutes to process this amazing declaration and what it means for you.

Pause and consider these questions:
- What are you afraid of?
- What keeps you from experiencing the joy of this good news?
- How can you find comfort in this news today?
- How could you share the comfort of this good news with those around you?

And the angel said to them,

"Fear not, for behold,

I bring you good news

of great joy that will be

for all the people."

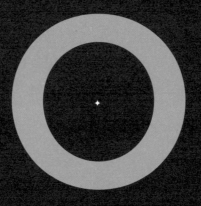

J O Y

TO THE

WORLD

1. Joy to the World, the Lord is come! Let earth re-ceive her King; —
2. Joy to the World, the Sa-vior reigns! Let men their songs em-ploy; —
3. No more let sins and sor-rows grow, Nor thorns in-fest the ground; —
4. He rules the world with truth and grace, And makes the na-tions prove —

— Let e-ver-y he-art pre-pa-re hi-m ro-om, And
— While fie-lds and___ flo-ods, rocks, hi-lls and___ plai-ns Re-
— He co-mes to___ ma-ke His ble-ss-ings flow___ Far
— The glo-ries___ of___ His righ-teous-ness___ And

Heaven and na-tu-re sing, And___ Heaven and na-tu-re
peat the soun-di-ing joy, Re - peat the soun-di-ing
as the curse is___ found, Far___ as the curse is___
won-ders of His___ love, And___ won-ders of His___

sing, And___ Hea-ven and Hea-ven and na-ture sing.
joy, Re - peat___ re-peat___ the soun-ding joy.
found, Far___ as___ Far as___ the curse is found.
love, And___ won-ders, And won - ders of his love.

• Lyrics: Isaac Watts
Music: George Frederick Handel; arr. Lowell Mason

20

TAKE A SECOND and think of all the titles people might attach to you. Some call you mother, father, brother, sister, aunt, uncle, nana, or grandfather. Others call you doctor, teacher, student, boss, coach, neighbor, or friend.

Today's passage is very important because of the titles that are attached to Jesus. These four titles speak volumes about who Jesus is. Did you catch them all? He's referred to as Savior, Christ, and Lord. He's also referred to as a baby. Each title carries significant meaning. The first three refer to his divine station and the last one speaks of his humble humanity.

There's much to be said about the humanity of Jesus. The fact that he came as a helpless baby by miraculous conception would by itself make him a historically unique figure. But Jesus came into a world that needed more than a virgin birth. While that was astounding, by itself it would be a headline that might mark history but not change it. Jesus was more than just an extraordinarily conceived baby.

He entered our world and lived a life like us. He understands our struggles and all that it means to be human. But Jesus came to a world that needed more than empathetic understanding. More than a reformer, a political leader, or another adviser, the world needed a Savior who is also Lord.

As you read the passage today, ask yourself which description of Jesus most resonates with how you relate to him. Is he a historical baby born long ago, or is he something more? Is Jesus your Savior? Is he your Lord?

For unto you
is born this day
in the city of David
a Savior, who is
Christ the Lord.
And this will be
a sign for you:
you will find
a baby wrapped
in swaddling
cloths and lying
in a manger.

CHRISTMAS TRIVIA

1 Where did Mary and Joseph live before Jesus was born?

2 What was the name of the angel that told the Virgin Mary she would have a child?

3 Why did Mary and Joseph go to Bethlehem?

4 Why couldn't Mary and Joseph find a place to stay?

5 Where did Mary lay the newborn baby Jesus? a) In a stable b) In hay c) In a manger

6 In which city was Jesus born?

7 What do the angels say together to the shepherds in praise to God?

8 How many wise men visited baby Jesus?

9 What gifts did the wise men bring for Jesus?

10 According to the Bible, which animals were specifically mentioned as being present in the stable when Jesus was born?

11 How many days after the birth of Christ did Joseph and Mary give him the name Jesus?

12 Who was the Roman ruler at the time Jesus was born?

READ
LUKE 2:13–14

And suddenly there was with the angel a multitude of the heavenly host praising God and saying, "Glory to God in the highest, and on earth peace among those with whom he is pleased!"

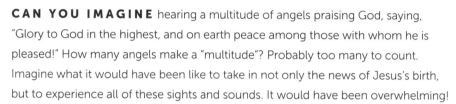

CAN YOU IMAGINE hearing a multitude of angels praising God, saying, "Glory to God in the highest, and on earth peace among those with whom he is pleased!" How many angels make a "multitude"? Probably too many to count. Imagine what it would have been like to take in not only the news of Jesus's birth, but to experience all of these sights and sounds. It would have been overwhelming!

And yet, even this would have been nothing more than a glimpse into how overwhelming it would be to experience the majesty of God. Remember when the Lord revealed himself to Moses? He hid Moses in a cleft of a rock until he passed by because "no one can see [God's] face and live" (see Exodus 33:20). Our human bodies here on earth physically can't handle the full presence of God. He is truly worthy of our praise.

This infinitely powerful God had just arrived on earth in the form of a helpless baby—fully human and fully God. He came to restore our relationship to God, but even more than this he came to bring glory to God. Christ was born to glorify God. Christ died to glorify God. Christ saves us to glorify God.

We were made to glorify him too! When we praise God for who he is, we are satisfied, settled, at peace, safe, and operating how we were wired to live now and forever.

If you're a follower of Christ, do you know that you appear in the Bible? And do you know what you're doing? You're praising God with the angels! At the end of the Bible, we get a glimpse into heaven, where God dwells among his people. Here's how John describes what God's people are doing: "[There is] a great multitude that no one could number, from every nation, from all tribes and peoples and languages, standing before the throne and before the Lamb" (Revelation 7:9) praising God with the angels. Who knows? Perhaps we'll be alongside the same group of angels from Luke 2.

This Christmas season, let's celebrate that God glorified himself by coming as a humble servant to die for us so that we can live in freedom and know this infinitely powerful God personally.

22

THERE ARE MANY LESSONS we can glean from these faithful shepherds. We've already seen God divinely interrupt the mundane duties of the shepherds with declarations of good news for all people. We pick up today with the same shepherds in the wake of a supernatural encounter. The angels are gone, and the shepherds are once again alone beneath a dark and desolate sky. And yet, something's very different this time. These unclean shepherds, near the bottom of the socioeconomic ladder, now have inside information: they know where Jesus was born!

Mary and Joseph gave a firsthand account of the birth of Christ. Zechariah and Elizabeth were told beforehand this would happen. But these lowly shepherds are the first to hear the news of the birth of Christ. Jesus has come to save his people from the penalty and power of sin and on this side of the story we get to see exactly how the shepherds respond.

Notice how the shepherds respond to the news that the Lord "made known" to them? They go with "haste" (2:16). What do they go "with haste" to do? They go to make "known the saying that had been told them concerning [Jesus]" (2:17). In other words, what God had made known to them they make known to others. The result? People "wondered" (2:18). This Christmas pray that God would give you opportunities to tell others about the Good News of Jesus. Pray also that they will respond with repentance and belief.

These faithful shepherds were the New Testament's first evangelists. This Christmas, pray that God would help you to follow in their footsteps. Pray that you might be bold to tell others about Jesus and that those who hear would be left to "wonder" as a result.

Be encouraged that as you share this great news with others, the angels in heaven are doing exactly what they were doing approximately 2,000 years ago on that very night, praising God for salvation.

Who should you share the gospel with this Christmas season? Spend some time praying and asking God who he has placed in your life specifically for this purpose.

When the angels went away from them into heaven, the shepherds said to one another, "Let us go over to Bethlehem and see this thing that has happened, which the Lord has made known to us." And they went with haste and found Mary and Joseph, and the baby lying in a manger. And when they saw it, they made known the saying that had been told them concerning this child. And all who heard it wondered at what the shepherds told them. But Mary treasured up all these things, pondering them in her heart. And the shepherds returned, glorifying and praising God for all they had heard and seen, as it had been told them. And at the end of eight days, when he was circumcised, he was called Jesus, the name given by the angel before he was conceived in the womb.

And when the time came for their purification according to the Law of Moses, they brought him up to Jerusalem to present him to the Lord (as it is written in the Law of the Lord, "Every male who first opens the womb shall be called holy to the Lord") and to offer a sacrifice according to what is said in the Law of the Lord, "a pair of turtledoves, or two young pigeons." Now there was a man in Jerusalem, whose name was Simeon, and this man was righteous and devout, waiting for the consolation of Israel, and the Holy Spirit was upon him. And it had been revealed to him by the Holy Spirit that he would not see death before he had seen the Lord's Christ. And he came in the Spirit into the temple, and when the parents brought in the child Jesus, to do for him according to the custom of the Law, he took him up in his arms and blessed God and said, "Lord, now you are letting your servant depart in peace, according to your word; for my eyes have seen your salvation that you have prepared in the presence of all peoples, a light for revelation to the Gentiles, and for glory to your people Israel."

23

SIMEON WAS RIGHTEOUS AND DEVOUT. He was a faithful Israelite who trusted God's Word, and he believed that the promised Messiah would come. But Simeon wasn't the only Israelite waiting for the Messiah. And there was something unique about Simeon's life: the Holy Spirit had revealed to him that he would not die until he'd seen the promised Savior.

Imagine this elderly man, full of the Holy Spirit, eagerly awaiting this very important day. And then it came! When Mary and Joseph brought Jesus into the temple, Simeon knew. He recognized Jesus as the One for whom he had been waiting. That's why he joyfully took the baby into his arms and blessed God. He could now face his own death in peace because he had seen his salvation in the flesh.

Simeon prayed, "My eyes have seen your salvation" (vs. 30). Notice, he didn't say, "My eyes have seen the One who we hope will bring salvation one day." He declared that Jesus is our salvation. Simeon could rest in peace at the end of his life because he was completely confident that salvation had come.

Do you ever feel like what you believe is uncertain? Do you ever feel like you're wandering in darkness waiting for someone to take the lead and just show you the way? If so, just as Simeon did, look to Jesus. Read what's revealed about him in God's Word—and choose to believe it. Notice how Jesus's life was prophesied long before his birth. Read the gospels and observe both his life and his teaching. To whom did Jesus talk? What did he say? Consider his life, death, and victorious resurrection.

Look to Jesus and trust in God's Word. If you believe in him, you will find peace throughout all the days of your life—just like Simeon.

24

OUR STUDY ENDS WITH ANNA, an old, widowed prophetess. When she sees Jesus, she gives thanks to God and can't help but speak to those who, like her, have been waiting for the redemption of Jerusalem. What a model of patient, persistent faith.

There's no better way to close out this devotional than to think through this past year and do the same.

Over the last year, what are some things you can thank God for? How has he provided for you? How did you feel cared for or seen by him? How has God answered a prayer or sustained you while you continue to pray for something he hasn't answered yet? What about him are you particularly grateful for this year (his grace, his authority, his creativity, etc.)? Write out your thoughts on the next page.

In the coming year, who can you pray for and share Jesus with? Think through places you frequent, people you live around, and people you may have known your whole life. On the next page write down their names and commit to pray for opportunities to share the gospel with them.

Challenge: Consider sharing what you've written here with friends, family, or your church family before the year is over!

And his father and his mother marveled at what was said about him. And Simeon blessed them and said to Mary his mother, "Behold, this child is appointed for the fall and rising of many in Israel, and for a sign that is opposed (and a sword will pierce through your own soul also), so that thoughts from many hearts may be revealed." And there was a prophetess, Anna, the daughter of Phanuel, of the tribe of Asher. She was advanced in years, having lived with her husband seven years from when she was a virgin, and then as a widow until she was eighty-four. She did not depart from the temple, worshiping with fasting and prayer night and day. And coming up at that very hour she began to give thanks to God and to speak of him to all who were waiting for the redemption of Jerusalem.

MY REFLECTION ON THE PAST YEAR

Read the devotion from Day 24. Reflect on God's provision over the past year and those things left unanswered. What about your relationship with God are you particularly grateful for as you look back over the year?

_____

_____

_____

_____

_____

_____

_____

_____

_____

_____

_____

_____

CONSIDER:

Who can I pray for and share Jesus with in the year ahead?

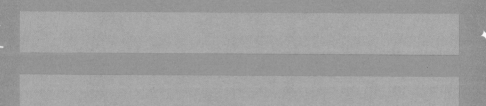

CH 1

CH 2

25

LUKE 1

¹ Inasmuch as many have undertaken to compile a narrative of the things that have been accomplished among us, ² just as those who from the beginning were eyewitnesses and ministers of the word have delivered them to us, ³ it seemed good to me also, having followed all things closely for some time past, to write an orderly account for you, most excellent Theophilus, ⁴ that you may have certainty concerning the things you have been taught.

⁵ In the days of Herod, king of Judea, there was a priest named Zechariah, of the division of Abijah. And he had a wife from the daughters of Aaron, and her name was Elizabeth. ⁶ And they were both righteous before God, walking blamelessly in all the commandments and statutes of the Lord. ⁷ But they had no child, because Elizabeth was barren, and both were advanced in years.

⁸ Now while he was serving as priest before God when his division was on duty, ⁹ according to the custom of the priesthood, he was chosen by lot to enter the temple of the Lord and burn incense. ¹⁰ And the whole multitude of the people were praying outside at the hour of incense. ¹¹ And there appeared to him an angel of the Lord standing on the right side of the altar of incense. ¹² And Zechariah was troubled when he saw him, and fear fell upon him.

¹³ But the angel said to him, "Do not be afraid, Zechariah, for your prayer has been heard, and your wife Elizabeth will bear you a son, and you shall call his name John. ¹⁴ And you will have joy and gladness, and many will rejoice at his birth, ¹⁵ for he will be great before the Lord. And he must not drink wine or strong drink, and he will be filled with the Holy Spirit, even from his mother's womb. ¹⁶ And he will turn many of the children of Israel to the Lord their God, ¹⁷ and he will go before him in the spirit and power of Elijah, to turn the hearts of the fathers to the children, and the disobedient to the wisdom of the just, to make ready for the Lord a people prepared."

¹⁸ And Zechariah said to the angel, "How shall I know this? For I am an old man, and my wife is advanced in years." ¹⁹ And the angel answered him, "I am Gabriel. I stand in the presence of God, and I was sent to speak to you and to bring you this good news. ²⁰ And behold, you will be silent and unable to speak until the day that these things take place, because you did not believe my words, which will be fulfilled in their time." ²¹ And the people were waiting for Zechariah, and they were wondering at his delay in the temple. ²² And when he came out, he was unable to speak to them, and they realized that he had seen a vision in the temple. And he kept making signs to them and remained mute. ²³ And when his time of service was ended, he went to his home.

²⁴ After these days his wife Elizabeth conceived, and for five months she kept herself hidden, saying, ²⁵ "Thus the Lord has done for me in the days when he looked on me, to take away my reproach among people."

²⁶ In the sixth month the angel Gabriel was sent from God to a city of Galilee named Nazareth, ²⁷ to a virgin betrothed to a man whose name was Joseph, of the house of David. And the virgin's name was Mary. ²⁸ And he came to her and said, "Greetings, O favored one, the Lord is with you!" ²⁹ But she was greatly troubled at the saying, and tried to discern what sort of greeting this might be. ³⁰ And the angel said to her, "Do not be afraid, Mary, for you have found favor with God. ³¹ And behold, you will conceive in your womb and bear a son, and you shall call his name Jesus. ³² He will be great and will be called the Son of the Most High. And the Lord God will give to him the throne of his father David, ³³ and he will reign over the house of Jacob forever, and of his kingdom there will be no end."

³⁴ And Mary said to the angel, "How will this be, since I am a virgin?"

³⁵ And the angel answered her, "The Holy Spirit will come upon you, and the power of the Most High will overshadow you; therefore the child to be born will be called holy—the Son of God. ³⁶ And behold, your relative Elizabeth in her old age has also conceived a son, and this is the sixth month with her who was called barren. ³⁷ For nothing will be impossible with God." ³⁸ And Mary said, "Behold, I am the servant of the Lord; let it be to me according to your word." And the angel departed from her.

³⁹ In those days Mary arose and went with haste into the hill country, to a town in Judah, ⁴⁰ and she entered the house of Zechariah and greeted Elizabeth.

⁴¹ And when Elizabeth heard the greeting of Mary, the baby leaped in her womb. And Elizabeth was filled with the Holy Spirit, ⁴² and she exclaimed with a loud cry, "Blessed are you among women, and blessed is the fruit of your womb! ⁴³ And why is this granted to me that the mother of my Lord should come to me? ⁴⁴ For behold, when the sound of your greeting came to my ears, the baby in my womb leaped for joy. ⁴⁵ And blessed is she who believed that there would be a fulfillment of what was spoken to her from the Lord."

⁴⁶ And Mary said, "My soul magnifies the Lord, ⁴⁷ and my spirit rejoices in God my Savior, ⁴⁸ for he has looked on the humble estate of his servant. For behold, from now on all generations will call me blessed; ⁴⁹ for he who is mighty has done great things for me, and holy is his name. ⁵⁰ And his mercy is for those who fear him from generation to generation. ⁵¹ He has shown strength with his arm; he has scattered the proud in the thoughts of their hearts; ⁵² he has brought down the mighty from their thrones and exalted those of humble estate; ⁵³ he has filled the hungry with good things, and the rich he has sent away empty. ⁵⁴ He has helped his servant Israel, in remembrance of his mercy, ⁵⁵ as he spoke to our fathers, to Abraham and to his offspring forever."

⁵⁶ And Mary remained with her about three months and returned to her home.

⁵⁷ Now the time came for Elizabeth to give birth, and she bore a son. ⁵⁸ And her neighbors and relatives heard that the Lord had shown great mercy to her, and they rejoiced with her. ⁵⁹ And on the eighth day they came to circumcise the child. And they would have called him Zechariah after his father, ⁶⁰ but his mother answered, "No; he shall be called John." ⁶¹ And they said to her, "None of your relatives is called by this name." ⁶² And they made signs to his father, inquiring what he wanted him to be called. ⁶³ And he asked for a writing tablet and wrote, "His name is John." And they all wondered. ⁶⁴ And immediately his mouth was opened and his tongue loosed, and he spoke, blessing God. ⁶⁵ And fear came on all their neighbors. And all these things were talked about through all the hill country of Judea, ⁶⁶ and all who heard them laid them up in their hearts, saying, "What then will this child be?" For the hand of the Lord was with him.

⁶⁷ And his father Zechariah was filled with the Holy Spirit and prophesied, saying, ⁶⁸ "Blessed be the Lord God of Israel, for he has visited and redeemed his people ⁶⁹ and has raised up a horn of salvation for us in the house of his servant David, ⁷⁰ as he spoke by the mouth of his holy prophets from of old, ⁷¹ that we should

be saved from our enemies and from the hand of all who hate us; [72] to show the mercy promised to our fathers and to remember his holy covenant, [73] the oath that he swore to our father Abraham, to grant us [74] that we, being delivered from the hand of our enemies, might serve him without fear, [75] in holiness and righteousness before him all our days. [76] And you, child, will be called the prophet of the Most High; for you will go before the Lord to prepare his ways, [77] to give knowledge of salvation to his people in the forgiveness of their sins, [78] because of the tender mercy of our God, whereby the sunrise shall visit us from on high [79] to give light to those who sit in darkness and in the shadow of death, to guide our feet into the way of peace."

[80] And the child grew and became strong in spirit, and he was in the wilderness until the day of his public appearance to Israel.

LUKE 2

[1] In those days a decree went out from Caesar Augustus that all the world should be registered. [2] This was the first registration when Quirinius was governor of Syria. [3] And all went to be registered, each to his own town. [4] And Joseph also went up from Galilee, from the town of Nazareth, to Judea, to the city of David, which is called Bethlehem, because he was of the house and lineage of David, [5] to be registered with Mary, his betrothed, who was with child. [6] And while they were there, the time came for her to give birth. [7] And she gave birth to her firstborn son and wrapped him in swaddling cloths and laid him in a manger, because there was no place for them in the inn.

[8] And in the same region there were shepherds out in the field, keeping watch over their flock by night. [9] And an angel of the Lord appeared to them, and the glory of the Lord shone around them, and they were filled with great fear. [10] And the angel said to them, "Fear not, for behold, I bring you good news of great joy that will be for all the people. [11] For unto you is born this

day in the city of David a Savior, who is Christ the Lord. [12] And this will be a sign for you: you will find a baby wrapped in swaddling cloths and lying in a manger." [13] And suddenly there was with the angel a multitude of the heavenly host praising God and saying, [14] "Glory to God in the highest, and on earth peace among those with whom he is pleased!"

[15] When the angels went away from them into heaven, the shepherds said to one another, "Let us go over to Bethlehem and see this thing that has happened,

which the Lord has made known to us." ¹⁶ And they went with haste and found Mary and Joseph, and the baby lying in a manger.

¹⁷ And when they saw it, they made known the saying that had been told them concerning this child. ¹⁸ And all who heard it wondered at what the shepherds told them. ¹⁹ But Mary treasured up all these things, pondering them in her heart. ²⁰ And the shepherds returned, glorifying and praising God for all they had heard and seen, as it had been told them.

²¹ And at the end of eight days, when he was circumcised, he was called Jesus, the name given by the angel before he was conceived in the womb.

²² And when the time came for their purification according to the Law of Moses, they brought him up to Jerusalem to present him to the Lord ²³ (as it is written in the Law of the Lord, "Every male who first opens the womb shall be called holy to the Lord") ²⁴ and to offer a sacrifice according to what is said in the Law of the Lord, "a pair of turtledoves, or two young pigeons." ²⁵ Now there was a man in Jerusalem, whose name was Simeon, and this man was righteous and devout, waiting for the consolation of Israel, and the Holy Spirit was upon him. ²⁶ And it had been revealed to him by the Holy Spirit that he would not see death before he had seen the Lord's Christ. ²⁷ And he came in the Spirit into the temple, and when the parents brought in the child Jesus, to do for him according to the custom of the Law, ²⁸ he took him up in his arms and blessed God and said, ²⁹ "Lord, now you are letting your servant depart in peace, according to your word; ³⁰ for my eyes have seen your salvation ³¹ that you have prepared in the presence of all peoples, ³² a light for revelation to the Gentiles, and for glory to your people Israel."

³³ And his father and his mother marveled at what was said about him. ³⁴ And Simeon blessed them and said to Mary his mother, "Behold, this child is appointed for the fall and rising of many in Israel, and for a sign that is opposed ³⁵ (and a sword will pierce through your own soul also), so that thoughts from many hearts may be revealed."

³⁶ And there was a prophetess, Anna, the daughter of Phanuel, of the tribe of Asher. She was advanced in years, having lived with her husband seven years from when she was a virgin, ³⁷ and then as a widow until she was eighty-four. She did not depart from the temple, worshiping with fasting and prayer night and day. ³⁸ And coming up at that very hour she began to give thanks to God and to speak of him to all who were waiting for the redemption of Jerusalem.

SCRAMBLE
ANSWERS (page 35)
TRUTH, EARTH, SOUNDING,
GLORIES, HEAVEN, REPEAT.
Final answer: RETURN.

WORD SEARCH
ANSWERS (page 43)

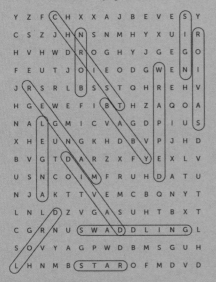

TRIVIA
ANSWERS (page 54)
1. Nazareth; 2. Gabriel;
3. To register for the census
(and possibly to pay taxes);
4. There was no room at the inn;
5. In a manger; 6. Bethlehem;
7. "Glory to God in the highest, and
on earth peace among those with
whom he is pleased"; 8. The Bible
doesn't say; 9. Gold, frankincense,
and myrrh; 10. None; 11. 8 days;
12. Caesar Augustus.

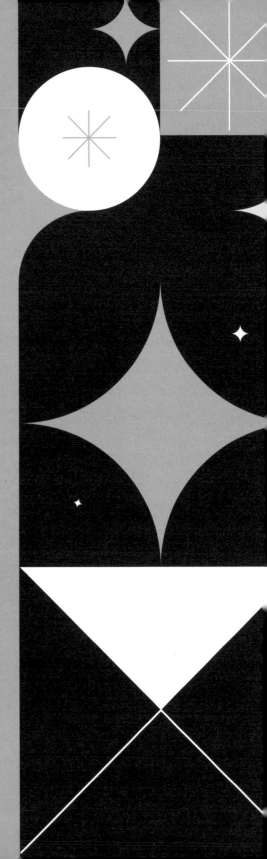

ELIZA HUIE, MA, LCPC

is the Director of Counseling at McLean Bible Church in Vienna, VA and author of several books. She teaches biblical counseling at Metro Baltimore Seminary and offers training and consulting to churches in areas related to counseling. Eliza and her husband have three grown children, two daughters-in-law, and the sweetest grandson!

CYNDI LOGSDON

and her husband have spent the past twenty years loving and serving the church around the world. They currently live in Istanbul, Turkey, where her husband serves as the pastor of an English-speaking church in a vibrant megacity. Cyndi and her husband have two grown daughters and a son-in-law.

BROOK TAYLOR

obtained a BA in Early Childhood Education before moving overseas with her family to plant churches in the Middle East. She's a pastor's wife, mom of five spirited boys, and a children's ministry director at McLean Bible Church.

ASHLEY AREY

is a creative who is passionate about the church and unleashing creativity in others. Her business focuses on upgrading building spaces, branding, graphic design, and strategic visual communication solutions. She currently resides in the Washington DC area with her husband and two sons, and is an advocate for adoption.